Can We Talk, God?

RICHARD ▼ DUNN

VICTOR BOOKS®
A DIVISION OF SCRIPTURE PRESS PUBLICATIONS INC.
USA CANADA ENGLAND

ABOUT THE AUTHOR

RICHARD DUNN is Chairman of the Youth Ministry Department at Trinity College in Deerfield, Illinois. He has over 10 years experience in youth ministry, and is a popular retreat and conference speaker as well as Youth Ministry Consultant for Lay Renewal Ministries of St. Louis, Missouri. Small group ministry is a primary focus as he disciples students and equips them for leadership.

All Bible quotations, unless otherwise indicated, are from the *Holy Bible, New International Version,* © 1973, 1978, 1984, International Bible Society. Used by permission of Zondervan Bible Publishers.

Library of Congress Catalog Card Number: 90-60253

ISBN: 0-89693-046-7

1 2 3 4 5 6 7 8 9 10 Printing/Year 94 93 92 91 90

© 1990, SP Publications, Inc. All rights reserved.
Printed in the United States of America.

CONTENTS

1 Where Are You?   5
God initiates a relationship with us and invites us to respond

2 Getting Better Acquainted   11
We can know God personally through His self-revelation

3 The Explorers   18
Practical ways to discover the transforming truth of God's Word

4 Teach Us How to Pray   25
The prayers of Paul and of Jesus guide us in communicating with God

5 Devotion — Not Just Devotions   31
Creative ideas for deepening our relationship with God

6 Burning Bright without Burning Out   38
Staying on fire with the help of Christian fellowship

ONE
▼

Where Are You?

♡ HEARTBEAT

"Where Are You?" begins a series of sessions which will help our group encourage and challenge one another to grow in a daily, personal relationship with God. Because each person in the group is an important part of our growth, let's start by understanding more about our relationships with God and one another.

So, what do you think? Take a moment to complete the following survey. Your ideas and experiences will be an important part of the group discussion in the BODYLIFE section.

Daily Devotions Survey
1. The concept that daily devotions/quiet times are an important part of being a Christian is one which _____.
  a. I always talk about on dates.
  b. I would talk about if I had a date.
  c. I have never heard about before today.
  d. I have heard teachers and/or speakers talk about.
  e. I have learned about and tried to apply to my own life.

2. When I think of daily devotions, the first thing I think about is:
    a. Falling asleep
    b. Singing hymns
    c. Reading the Bible
    d. Praying
    e. Memorizing Scripture
    f. Worship
    g. Other _____

3. I think that I _____ friends who daily participate in some of the things listed in number two.
    a. do not have any
    b. have one or two
    c. have several
    d. have many

4. At this point in my life I feel that daily devotions (you may choose more than one answer) _____.
    a. are necessary for me to begin or continue doing.
    b. would be a nice thing to do, but are not necessary.
    c. are not a priority for me to think about.
    d. are a priority, but one which I have trouble doing.
    e. are a priority which I already maintain consistently.

5. When I think about my daily relationship with God, the strongest feeling that I experience is:
    a. Frustration
    b. Guilt
    c. Indifference
    d. Fear
    e. Joy
    f. Excitement
    g. Confusion
    h. All of the above!
    i. Other _____

LIFELINE

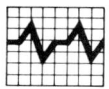

In Genesis, God seems to be looking for Adam as if He has lost him. Consider for a moment why God asked, "Adam, where are you?" It is not likely that God could not see around trees or that He was playing hide and seek. What are some possible reasons we could list for why God would have asked this question of Adam?

Working in cell groups of two or three persons, examine together Genesis 3:6-13. God was surely able to see where Adam was and had not physically lost him. But there was a sense of loss in the relationship God had with Adam. After reading this passage, discuss in your cell groups what seems to you to have been "lost."

As a total group, let's finish this sentence based on our understanding of the passage: It seems that God asked Adam, "Where are you?" because. . . .

Adam must have been experiencing some very strong emotions when he was hiding from God. Circle the two emotions that you would have been feeling most strongly.

anger	shame	excitement
sadness	fear	anxiety
hurt	joy	disappointment
guilt	happiness	embarassment

Now underline the two emotions which you think would best describe God's feelings at this point.

Adam's sin had resulted in terrible consequences. God disciplined Adam and Eve because they violated His will for them in Eden. Still, even after this violation, God kept seeking a relationship with Adam. What does this tell you about God's attitude toward Adam?

To what extent would God go to in order to restore what had been lost? This can be answered by examining what God has done to bring us into a relationship with Him.

Missing Person: You
Please read the following statements and answer them according to the Scriptures listed.

(True/False)   I have sinned against God just as Adam did (Romans 3:23).
(True/False)   God offers me His love because I promise to be good (Romans 5:8).
(True/False)   I am so valuable to God that He searched for me when I was lost in sin (Matthew 18:12-14).

As a group, let's complete this sentence:
God has shown that He wants a personal relationship with us by. . . .

BODYLIFE
God removes the curse of sin and gives us eternal life in Christ. This restores part of what was lost in Eden. But God also wants to restore that daily relationship destroyed by sin. God values a relationship with you.

How can we enjoy that daily relationship? Perhaps you have heard Christians talk about having "daily devotions" or "quiet times." As a group, let's review our answers to the surveys and explore the feelings and/or experiences we have in common concerning the topic of daily devotions.

God seeks a personal, daily relationship with you. He values your taking the time and the effort required to build that relationship. He is not so concerned about your having "daily devotions" as He is concerned about your having a daily devotion to Him.

Lost and Found

Given that God has provided Christ for your salvation and that God continues to seek a daily relationship with you, how is your relationship with God growing? God asked Adam, "Where are you?"

How would you respond if God asked you, "Where are you?"

Where Are You?

If your daily personal life with God were compared to being in the garden, how would you describe this relationship?
   a. I am walking close by God's side, talking with Him daily.
   b. Some days I feel close to His side, other days I feel like I cannot find where He is.
   c. Some days I feel close to His side, other days I feel like I am just too tired to keep walking with Him.
   d. I used to walk close to His side, but lately it seems as if we are always in different parts of the garden.
   e. I feel lost in the garden and, even though I can hear God's voice calling for me, I cannot seem to find my way back to Him.
   f. I feel like I have been hiding from God because I do not know how He feels about me right now.
   g. I feel lost in the garden and I feel that God is not really calling out to me anymore.

Life Response
God wants you right where you are! Read Jeremiah 29:13. What is the promise found here?

Based on that promise, let's work together as a group to support one another in our commitment to respond to our seeking God this next week. A space is provided for you to write your individual commitment to respond in one specific way this week to God's seeking of a personal relationship with you. Try to make your commitment
- measurable ("I will read my Bible and pray each day this week" instead of "I will be more faithful in my devotions")
- realistic ("I will devote at least 10 minutes to my time alone with God" instead of "I will read through the entire Bible in a week.")

COMMITMENT

In response to the God who seeks me, I commit that I will. . . .

Signed, _____

What's Next?
"Getting Better Acquainted" — How can you get to know God on a more personal level?

T W O
▼

Getting Better Acquainted

♡ HEARTBEAT
Hike of Your Life

Fill in the blanks on the "Hike of Your Life" map on the next page. If your life were a hike, where would this last week have led you? Would it have been a valley? A mountain? A resting place?

We are continuing on our group's adventure of learning to experience God in our daily lives. We will be getting to know one another more personally as our journey together leads us to get to know more personally the God who seeks us.

Working through the Hike of Your Life helps us to know each other better. But how do we come to know God more personally? How can we really know more *of* God instead of just knowing more *about* Him?

As a group, let's name some of the things that seem to make it difficult for people, especially your friends, to know God personally.

CAN WE TALK, GOD?

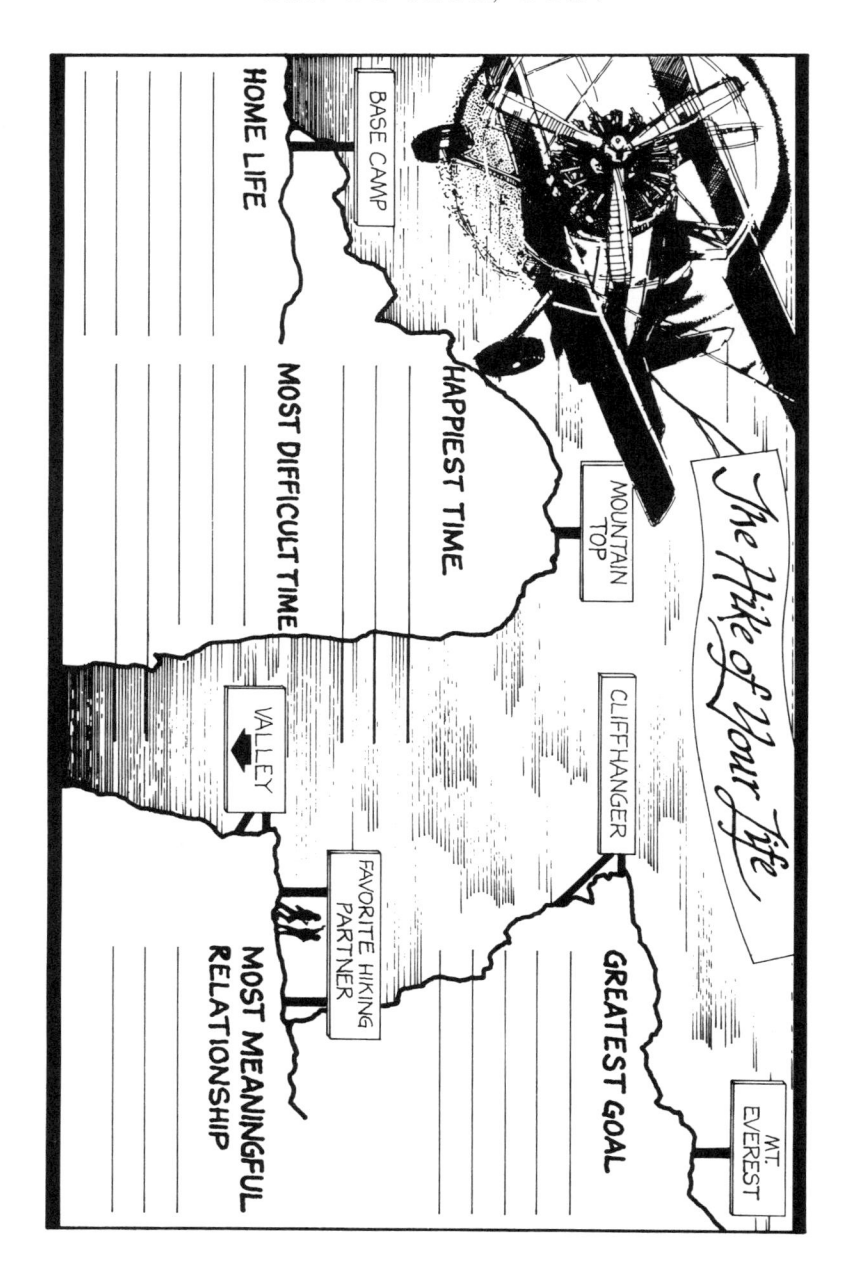

LIFELINE

When it come to knowing God, there are many different approaches. Some people try to use their logic to come to an intellectual conclusion on who He is. Others try to understand Him based on their experiences. Others feel like they can only guess at who He must be. But God is not available to us by our efforts alone. You cannot be 100 percent certain about God unless He chooses to let you know Him.

Theologians describe this characteristic of God as His "transcendence." In other words, God is beyond us. He cannot be seen or touched or heard whenever we want to see, touch, or hear Him. He is beyond our human capabilities. For this reason, the God who seeks us makes Himself known to us by His "revelation." He has chosen for you to know Him! The word "revelation" means "uncovering." In other words, God "took the lid off" to show us what we could not know by ourselves.

God has revealed Himself in different ways. Let's examine the ways in which we can begin to know the "beyond" God in a personal way.

Creation

Let's read Romans 1:20. What can be known about God from His Creation?

Read silently Psalm 19:1-6. These verses tell us that Creation reveals God. What are some ways in which Creation helps you believe in, understand, or know more about God?

Miracles

God is not only revealed in the natural created order, but also in His supernatural acts as well. Check out these verses in which Stephen describes a few of God's miraculous works in his defense before the high priest: Acts 7:2-47. After reading through these verses as a group, discuss the questions listed below.

1. What are some of God's miracles found in this review?

2. What do you learn about God through these supernatural acts and events?

3. Stephen says in verses 51-53 that the religious leaders had rejected Jesus just as they had all the prophets before. Read these verses and discuss the difference between knowing about God through revelation and actually knowing and obeying Him as God.

Jesus

Jesus as the incarnation (God in the flesh) is also God's revelation of Himself. Read John 1:1-4, John 14:9-11, and Hebrews 1:1-4. Based on these verses, do you agree or disagree with the following statement? Why or why not?

Jesus is a unique revelation of God. (Agree/Disagree)

So you can know the transcendent God because He has revealed Himself, right? Time out! Natural revelation teaches us *about* God, but we cannot really know Him through Creation alone. And who in our group has ever heard a burning bush talk or seen a local river parted or witnessed some other supernatural revelation of God? Furthermore, who of us has actually, physically seen Jesus? Is revelation of any real help to us? How can we know for sure who God is if these are not clearly visible to us as they were to Moses or to Stephen or to the disciples?

God's Word
God has not left us without revelation of Himself that is specific and available to us all the time. Just as Stephen spoke with confidence on the things of Moses without seeing Moses, we can know the things of Moses, Stephen, and, most important, of Jesus through the revealed written Word of the Scriptures.

Two very important verses which the apostles Paul and Peter wrote are 2 Timothy 3:16 and 2 Peter 1:20-21. After reading these verses, what reason would you give for our confidence that Scripture truly is God's revelation of Himself?

God's Spirit
The Spirit of God breathed (inspired) the authors of the Bible to write His truth. This same Spirit is alive and working, though in a different way, to reveal God in the life of every Christian.

Read John 14:16 and John 15:26. What does the Spirit do for us as believers in Jesus Christ?

BODYLIFE
With His Word to reveal His truth to us and His Spirit to guide us into a personal experience of that truth, we have been given a revelation of God that enables us to know Him personally and experience a meaningful relationship with Him on a daily basis. The "lid" has been taken off so that we may encounter God personally.

What has been revealed to us as individuals? What have we come to know in our relationship with God? To begin to answer these questions, let's list all that we can know to be true about God.

This is our testimony of how God has been active in our lives to reveal Himself to us. God has revealed Himself to us in the Bible and He makes that revelation real to us by the Spirit. We want to continue to respond to His revelation so that we can know and experience more of this on a daily basis.

Life Response
Which of the qualities or attributes we listed would you like to experience more personally on a daily basis?

Based on what we are learning together about revelation, how can we begin to specifically and personally know more of God and His qualities in our daily lives?

Let's commit ourselves to (1) making one specific and personal response to His revelation this week and (2) praying for one another's daily relationship with God.

What's Next?
"The Explorers" — How can you personally discover more of who God is through His Word?

THREE

▼

The Explorers

♡ HEARTBEAT

We are continuing to explore how we can communicate with and know God more personally. Our next step is to examine how we can develop and deepen our specific, personal responses to the revelation God has provided us. To begin, let's brainstorm all the possible attitudes and feelings (positive and negative) people have toward the Bible.

Check four attitudes/feelings from the brainstorm list which best describe your perspective on the Bible.

Now circle the two which most accurately describe your experience with the Bible this last week.

THE EXPLORERS

LIFELINE

David

In "cell groups" of two or three, read aloud Psalm 119:1-16. Then answer the following questions.

1. How many different words does the poet use to refer to God's Word?

2. Describe the poet's attitude toward God's Word.

3. What are some of the ways the writer responds to God's word?

4. If you were to ask the writer of this psalm, "Why is God's word so important to you?" how do you think he would reply?

Jesus

In those same groups, read Matthew 5:17-19; John 5:39; and John 17:17.

1. Describe Jesus' attitude about the Law and the Prophets (Old Testament Scriptures).

2. Why are these Old Testament Scriptures important when it comes to knowing Jesus?

3. What seemed to be the mistake of the Pharisees when they read God's word?

4. Rewrite John 17:17 in your own words.

5. How would you summarize Jesus' attitude about God's revealed Word?

Paul

In your cell groups, briefly examine Paul's attitude expressed in 2 Timothy 3:14-17 and the attitude of the author of Hebrews (possibly Paul) in Hebrews 4:12. After reading each passage aloud, use these questions to reflect on the verses.

1. What attitude did Paul want Timothy to have toward the Scriptures?

2. Paul was confident that God's Word could have an important role in Timothy's life. What are some of the ways in which the Scriptures could be useful to Timothy?

3. As a group, rewrite Hebrews 4:12 so that someone at your school who was not familiar with the Bible or biblical language could understand what it means.

Personal Conclusions

Based on this LIFELINE section, I would have to say that the Bible is (necessary, important, helpful, unimportant) for a Christian because. . . .

BODYLIFE

The Bible becomes real when it is studied as both *true* and *transforming*. It is God's absolute truth, and it can transform you by His Spirit into more of the person God created you to be.

Sometimes, though, it's difficult to know how to read the Bible to really get something out of it. As a group, we are going to experience a method for learning and growing through just a few minutes of personal Bible reading a day. It's called the PROACT method for Bible study.

PROACT stands for:

Pray — Ask the God who seeks and reveals to make Himself known to you through His Word.

Read — Read the verses just before and just after the passage. Now read the passage to understand what the author wanted the reader to know.

Observe — What truth is there to be known? Is there a command, a parable, an example, a principle, a new insight, etc.?

Apply — What is one specific way in which you could apply this truth in your own daily life?

Commit — Commit yourself to respond to this truth revealed by God. Ask Him for the strength and wisdom of His Spirit to be real to you as you seek to know Him more by doing His will.

Thank — Express thanksgiving to God for the revelation of His Word and the presence of His Spirit.

PROACT Practice

Scripture Passage:

Pray: Seek God and a knowledge of His Truth.

Read: Read the passage and the verses just before and after.

Observe: Write the main truth which you have learned from the passage. (Is it a command, a new insight, an example, an attitude, etc.?)

Apply: I can respond to this truth in my own life by. . . .

Commit: I choose to respond to this truth by . . .

recognizing that I can do this only through His Spirit.

Thank: Personal praise to God. Write out your thanksgiving for God's revelation and for His Spirit's presence with you as you respond to this truth.

Life Response

COMMITMENT

My commitment to God's transforming truth this next week:

What's Next
"Teach Us How to Pray" — How can you deepen your personal communication with God?

FOUR

▼

Teach Us How to Pray

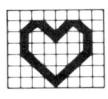

❤ HEARTBEAT

An important part of a daily personal relationship with God is prayer. All relationships, whether with parents, teammates, leaders, or friends, require communication if they are to be worthwhile. Our relationship with God is no exception. And it is prayer which is the key to quality communication with God.

What about your prayers? Answer the following questions so that we can discuss how our communication with God is at this point in our lives. Remember, there are no wrong answers!

1. Most of my prayers to God concern . . .

grades	personal issues
dates	family problems
wanting to know His will	things I need
forgiveness	others' needs
praise to Him	personal doubts
my need for guidance	my need for help
other:	

2. This past week I...
    prayed at a specific time each day
    just prayed whenever I thought of it
    prayed only before exams or before I asked to borrow the car or some other scary event
    prayed only when I was at church
    prayed maybe once or twice but I don't remember now
    did not pray at all
    never even thought of praying
    other:

3. I would say that overall my communication with God last week was...
    GREAT!
    good!
    OK
    there
    not there
    YUCK!

4. A good prayer for me is one which....

Take a few moments to pray as a group that God would teach you more about what it means to communicate with Him.

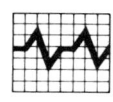

LIFELINE

Divide into smaller "cell groups" with each group taking one of the passages listed below as your prayer to study.

A. Ephesians 3:14-21
B. Philippians 1:9-11
C. Colossians 1:9-13

In your cell groups, answer the following questions about the prayer Paul prayed for the people in that church:

1. What were Paul's requests for the people?

2. How does Paul seem to view God according to these prayers? How is He described or addressed by Paul?

3. What does Paul see as God's will for these people?

4. What does Paul praise God for?

5. From this prayer, what would you say is Paul's attitude about prayer?

Praying can sometimes be like going shopping. We have a list of items we present to God asking Him to bless them or to fill our need for them. Obviously, there is nothing wrong with asking God for blessings or to meet our needs, but Paul's prayers seem to be more than presenting God with a shopping list.

In the whole group, summarize, based on your smaller group studies, the important characteristics that you observed in Paul's prayers.

Jesus' Pattern of Prayer for Ourselves

Jesus' disciples asked Him to teach them how to pray. He responded by giving them what we now call "The Lord's Prayer." What important characteristics do you find in Jesus' prayer that he taught His disciples as it is recorded in Matthew 6:9-13?

After looking at the prayer given by Jesus to the disciples and the prayers written by Paul on behalf of the churches, what seem to be the important characteristics we are to have in our prayers if we are to follow the examples of Jesus and Paul?

Prayerful Confidence

Prayer is the opportunity for us to participate with God in His accomplishment of His will in our lives and the lives of others. Prayers can be made with confidence because the One we are praying to is our God.

Read Matthew 7:7-11 to find out why Jesus said we could be confident about our prayers for our needs. Then read 1 Thessalonians 5:23-24 to see why Paul was confident that God would answer his prayers for others.

Summarize what you discovered as you read these passages.

BODYLIFE

As a group, let's discuss prayer in the context of the verses we just read.

1. We should pray because. . . .

2. If we do not pray we. . . .

3. In what ways is prayer important for our communication with God?

Life Response
In obedience to God, let's pray for His will to be accomplished in our own lives and in the lives of one another this week. First, let's make a list of our individual needs and write them down so that we can pray for God's will for our specific needs. Our commitment will be to pray about these needs for ourselves as we seek our Father's provisions.

Now let's write out a prayer for the group itself that we can pray during this week. This prayer can be patterned after the prayers of Paul and will become our group prayer.

What's Next?
"Devotion—Not Just Devotions"—What if your devotions get boring?

FIVE
▼

Devotion — Not Just Devotions

♥ HEARTBEAT

Someone once said that the way children spell "love" is T-I-M-E. Most likely all of us understand love in this way. If we love a person we will take the time to get to know that person. That's because if love is to grow it must be shared.

Our relationship with God needs time in order to grow as well. There is no such thing as "Microwave" Christianity or "Freeze-Dried Instant" love for God. We have a personal relationship with a seeking, revealing God who wants to be in intimate communication with us.

This group time is for the purpose of encouraging and helping one another spend more quality relationship-building time with God. As we continue our journey together toward a better personal walk with God, let's look at what it means to have an intimate relationship in our lives.

For parts 1 and 3 divide into smaller "cell groups" of two to four people. For part 2 work together as a whole group.

CAN WE TALK, GOD?

1. (In cell groups) Your small group has been given the task of designing the perfect friend. Please be specific about the characteristics and personal qualities which the perfect friend would possess. In a few moments you will present these to the large group.

2. (As a whole group) Share your description of the perfect friend. Which of the qualities of a perfect friend does God possess? In what ways can it be said that knowing God is like having a best friend? In what ways is it different?

3. (In cell groups) Using the word "RELATIONSHIP" as an acrostic, write out what it is like to have God as a friend. (Each sentence will start with the letter listed.) Be prepared to share your ideas with the whole group.

DEVOTION — NOT JUST DEVOTIONS

R

E

L

A

T

I

O

N

S

H

I

P

LIFELINE

Spending time building a relationship with God can involve many areas of your life. In fact, all of your life can be lived with an awareness of His presence and love for you.

We have been looking at how prayer and Bible study build our intimacy with God. Let's examine some verses to discover other ways in which God can be experienced as real.
- Psalm 119:48
- Psalm 149:2-5
- Psalm 150:3-5
- 2 Corinthians 9:6-8
- 1 Peter 4:10-11

Read aloud these mini-biographies of students who are experiencing God in their daily lives. Then answer these two questions on your own.

1. Which one of these examples appeals to me the most? Why does this best fit my style of relating?

2. How could I realistically apply this example to my own life? What types of things would I be doing to be consistent in my daily walk with God if I applied this example next week?

A. Teresa loves to have quiet, alone time to focus her thoughts on God every morning. She eats her breakfast and then reads a short passage from a devotional guide. After about five minutes of reading, she takes time to write her thoughts and a prayer for the day in her journal. When she has finished this quality time with God, she feels refreshed and ready to spend her day with God close by.

DEVOTION – NOT JUST DEVOTIONS

B. Nathan likes to try a lot of variety in his relationship with God. He journals a few days each month, memorizes at least one passage of Scripture each week, and meets with three other guys from church to pray after school on Tuesdays and Thursdays. Most of his Bible study centers on the small group Bible study he meets with weekly.

C. Lauren likes to approach her relationship with God in a very organized manner. She is currently working on a daily set of readings which will enable her to read through the Bible in one year. She keeps a notebook which includes daily PROACT sheets and a prayer journal. She always uses the first few moments of her homework time in the evening so that she can reflect on the day in this Bible study and begin her school work with a positive attitude.

D. Jacob loves music and often takes his time alone with God to sing hymns, read Scripture, meditate, and worship. He usually begins with a praise song; then, using the PROACT method, he meditates on God's Word, finishing with prayer and a song of thanksgiving. Jacob writes creative, new lyrics to familiar tunes to express his love for God.

E. Katie has her day divided into three times with God. She takes a few moments each morning to read the Bible and write some notes in her journal. During the day she tries to find a way to apply the truth she has learned. Her second time with God is during study hall, when she takes 10 minutes to pray. Later, in the evening, she writes in her journal any applications she has made with the truth she has learned and also any prayers she has seen God answer.

F. Jessica loves to spend time with people. She often volunteers her time to serve the needs of children as well as the elderly. She also is very sensitive to her friends, always there to listen and support and pray for them. Jessica reads from her Bible daily during the time she has set aside to pray for her friends that she wants to share God's love with. On her way to be with a friend or to spend time with an elderly person, instead of having the radio on in the car, she uses that time to ask God to take care of the person she is going to be with and to help her share His love with that person.

BODYLIFE

Based on our study and discussion together, let's list as many possible ways we can think of in which we can spend time with God developing our personal relationship with Him. The list can include specific ways to be involved in Bible study, prayer, worship, service, and all ideas we can come up with that would apply. Let's be specific and creative!

Life Response
From the list we just made, choose one way in which you want to introduce some creativity or consistency into your friendship with God. It may be something creative you have never tried before or it may be a way in which you are already coming to know and experience God more, but you need to develop consistency.

Outline exactly how you will apply this in the next week and be ready to share in our next meeting how your application contributed to your relationship with God.

MY APPLICATION:
What?
When?
How?

What's Next?
"Burning Bright without Burning Out"—How can you keep your journey with God from becoming a dead end?

SIX

Burning Bright without Burning Out

HEARTBEAT
As a group we have explored how God reveals Himself, opening the way for us to communicate with Him. We have also examined the need for consistency and creativity in our response to the relationship He offers to us on a daily basis. We close out this series with a look at how Christian community is an important part of our maintaining creative and consistent communication with our God.

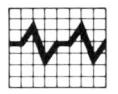

LIFELINE
We are going to look at a community experience found in the Bible in which Christians joined together to "feed" one another literally and figuratively.

First, let's do a word association. Write out all the words you can think of when the leader says, "_____."

In cell groups of two to four, read Acts 2:42-47. List all the important activities of this early experiment in community and then discuss this question:
- What were the things which seemed most important to these people?

This passage in Acts is the beginning of Christ's disciples coming together as a Christian community to minister the Gospel He had left for them to preach and teach. From this came the organization we call our local church.

Based on this first church, complete the following sentences in your cell group.

1. The purpose of the church is (Ephesians 4:11-16 may give some added insights). . . .

2. The community of Christian fellowship is important to the Christian's life because (Hebrews 10:22-23 may give some added insights). . . .

Based on these passages, let's discuss as a whole group which things listed in our word association seem to be essential aspects of the church as a community of fellowship. Put a check mark by those that qualify.

Complete this sentence: "The church is a place of Christian fellowship and community when...."

BODYLIFE

Christ intended for us to grow through our coming together as a community where His Spirit would not only be present in each individual but also as an active participant in the group.

A friend in the youth group asks, "Why do I need to be involved in a fellowship group in order to know God better?" Write a 50- to 75-word response based on the verses you studied above and your experience in this small group. Be prepared to share your response with others in the group.

Keep the Fire Burning!

In order to keep a fire burning you need heat and fuel. But you also need oxygen. A hot fire will extinguish immediately if there is no oxygen in its environment to sustain the flames.

As one who has been seeking to know God on a personal level and on a daily basis, you have been adding heat and fuel to the fire of your love for God. To continue in this you need to keep yourself in an atmosphere of Christian fellowship which will fan the flames.

We have spent time responding and sharing together in response to the God who seeks, reveals, and communicates Himself to us so that we may share His love daily. We have worked together to experience creativity, consistency, and community in our personal spiritual growth.

Life Response

As we close, let's discuss what specific commitments we will make to continue this growth in our lives.

COMMITMENT

I commit to being a part of experiencing Christian community so that I may continue to grow as a member of Christ's Body and in my daily communication with God. I will do this by. . . .

GROUP MEMBER EVALUATION
Can We Talk, God?

Please take a minute to fill out and mail this form giving us your candid reaction to this book. Thanks for your help!

Did you enjoy this book? Why or why not?

How has this book helped you . . .
- grow closer to your group?

- grow closer to God?

Do you plan to use other SonPower Small Group Studies?

In what setting did you use this book? (circle one)

Sunday School   Youth group   Midweek Bible study

Other:_____

How many members were in your group?

What grade are you in?

(OPTIONAL)
　　　　　Name _____

　　　　　Address _____

　　　　　　　　　 _____

PLACE
STAMP
HERE

Sonpower Youth Sources Editor
Victor Books
1825 College Avenue
Wheaton, Illinois 60187